THIS NOTEBOOK BELONGS TO:

Made in the USA
Monee, IL
28 April 2022

95522298R00059